God Even Made the Birds and the Bees

Rosemary Simmons Ellsworth

Illustrated by Lee Highgate

WestBow Press books may be ordered through booksellers or by contacting:

WestBow Press
A Division of Thomas Nelson & Zondervan
1663 Liberty Drive
Bloomington, IN 47403
www.westbowpress.com
844-714-3454

Interior Image Credit: Lee Highgate

ISBN: 978-1-6642-5175-5 (sc)
ISBN: 978-1-6642-5176-2 (e)

Library of Congress Control Number: 2021924451

Print information available on the last page.

WestBow Press rev. date: 01/07/2022

WESTBOW
P R E S S®
A DIVISION OF THOMAS NELSON
& ZONDERVAN

Acknowledgment

To my mom, Jean, and my dad, James, who is in heaven now. You raised me in the church since birth, setting a wonderful example of trusting and serving God, for your three children. Mom, you have encouraged me for years to use my talent for words to write a book, although I'm not sure whether this is the one you expected. I hope this is the first of many to come. Thank you for always believing in me and encouraging me.

To my husband, Scott, thank you for loving me, being the blessing God sent me, and sharing in God's creation of our three wonderful children. God has given each of them his or her own path of service. May all of them always keep their trust in and eyes on God and follow Him faithfully.

To my twin sister, Sarah, who shared this journey of creation with me and has always been my biggest support. Thank you for everything you have done for me and my family over the years. God knew I needed you and supplied that need from the beginning.

To Lee, thank you for agreeing to help me bring this book to life with your God-given artistic gift for illustrating.

Last but never least, I want to thank God for His direction in my life. No matter what I have gone through or had to face, God has always been there for me, taking care of me, guiding me, teaching me, and protecting me. I am so thankful for just a glimpse into how God uses us to bring forth the blessings of His beautiful babies.

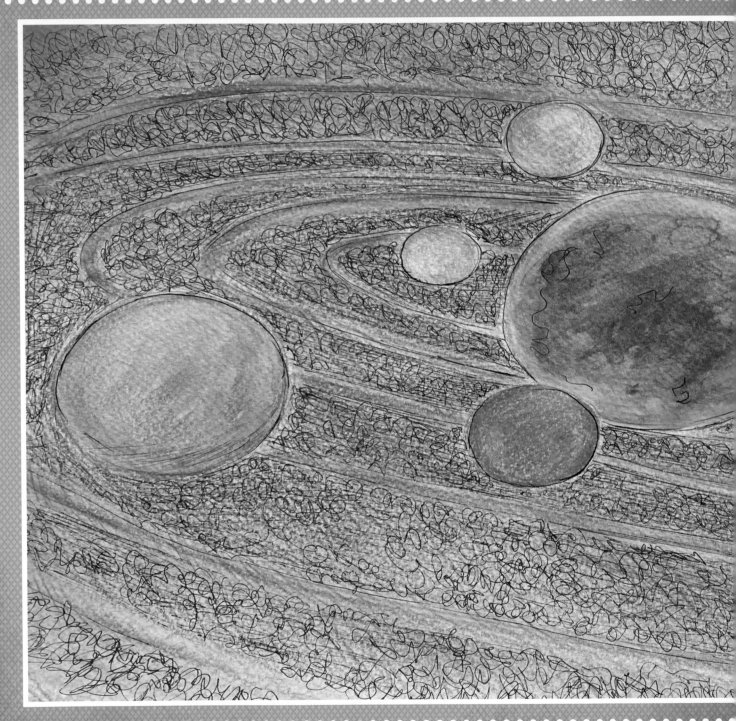

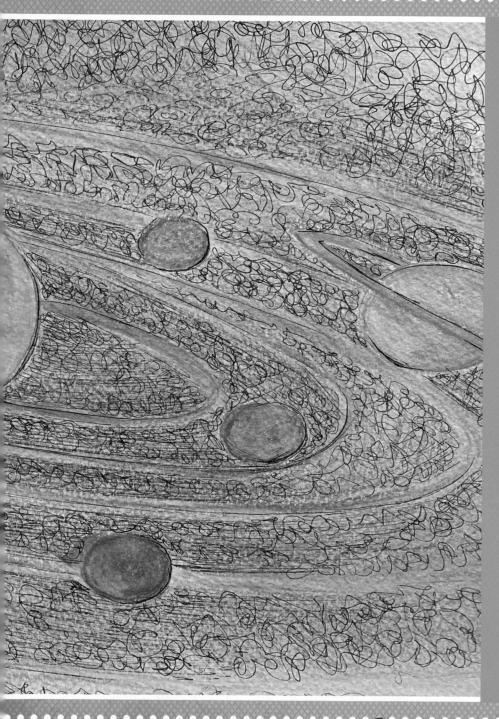

God created the
heavens, the
earth, the moon,
and the stars.

God made all the animals, the trees, the water, and the fish.
God made you, and He made me.
God even made the birds and the bees!

By now, you may know that you came from inside your mom's belly. You may have even seen her belly get bigger and bigger with a little brother or sister growing inside. But how did we get in there?

God placed each one of us in there!

Just as God provides all the necessary things to grow a seed into a flower or a tree, He also provides Moms and Dads with all the parts needed to make you and me.

Just as God has made many different types of people, there are many varieties of seeds. Some grow apples, oranges, or corn, while others grow coconuts or even dandelions. The one thing they all have in common is they start out as small seeds.

God makes a way for the seed to get to a place where it can be planted. He uses bees collecting nectar and pollen to travel from flower to flower, leaving pollen behind and fertilizing the plants as they go. Birds collect seeds to eat. They drop some of them over large areas of earth. The seeds eventually find their way into the soil; sometimes insects bury them, or our feet press them down into the dirt as we walk on it!

God then allows the rain to fall, the sun to shine, and nutrients in the ground to soften the seed's shell. The plant starts growing, safe and protected under the ground until it is strong enough to push through the soil to the surface above. God continues to bless it with the sun, rain, and nutrients to feed the plant as it grows into a healthy tree or plant, bearing the fruit God intended it to bear. With the strong roots He provides, that plant grows strong and stays rooted in the ground come wind or heavy rain. Our parents are to keep us rooted in God's word so when the storms of life arise, we are not uprooted and tossed about, but stand firm with our trust in God and His provision for our lives.

Whether an apple, orange, corn, coconut, or dandelion, God has a specific purpose for each one.

God will always prepare us for the tasks he has for us to complete!

Equip you with everything good that you may do his will, working in us that which is pleasing in his sight, through Jesus Christ, to whom be glory forever and ever. Amen (Hebrews 13:21 ESV).

God does the same with our parents. He gives a girl many tiny eggs, or seeds, inside her belly. As she grows from a little girl to reach puberty (the physical changing of her body to mature adult functions), God begins preparing her body for the day He will allow a baby to grow inside her.

Changes happen such as growing hair in her armpits and on her genital (private) area and starting her period (menstrual cycle) each month. This is when an egg, like the seed of a plant, is stored in the ovaries (two tiny organs to hold all the eggs). One egg is released from the organ about every twenty-eight days. If the egg is not fertilized and does not become a baby, it will break down with the lining of the uterus (the place the baby grows in) into a bloody liquid. This liquid will leak out of a woman's body through her vagina (the tunnel to the outside of her body) for a few days each month. This is called her period. After her period, the cycle begins again until the next month.

She also begins to develop breasts. This will allow her to feed the baby milk it needs to grow until big enough to eat solid foods. God made her body curvy and soft to store extra nutrients to support her while she carries the baby inside her. We all remember the kisses, soft hugs, and love our mothers gave to us when they were finally able to hold us in their arms.

God prepares a boy's body to mature to puberty with armpit hair, leg hair, and genital hair. He begins producing the fertilizer known as sperm in his testes (small organs like the ovaries in females). Sperm are like little tadpoles that swim around in a slippery liquid called semen (a nutrient substance for sperm). There are millions of sperm in this cloudy white liquid. With the increase in hormones (chemical substances that carry messages to help cells work) during puberty, boys find their penises can leak this liquid at times while they are sleeping. This is known as a wet dream or nocturnal emissions. Girls can experience a similar reaction during sleep.

The sperm are produced by the testicles. Fluids are added along the path to feed the sperm and allow them to move easier in the semen. God also starts males' bodies to grow big and strong. When they become dads, they protect us, carry us around, provide for us, and care for us as we grow, once we are in the outside world.

God designed the reproduction of all plants, trees, fish, crabs, insects, and even the birds and the bees.

How amazing He is!

God thought of it all! He designed every part and planned how each function to create more beings.

And you, be fruitful and multiply, increase greatly on the earth and multiply in it (Genesis 9:7 ESV).

Now we will skip ahead to after Mom and Dad have found each other, are married, and feel they are ready to start their own family together.

God blesses them to be in love, happy, and attracted to each other. In the hours leading up to bedtime, they look at each other, smile, giggle, and talk very sweetly to each other—more than at regular times in the day. This is a special time for them to show how much they appreciate having each other and how much love they have for each other throughout the marriage.

Once in bed, they give each other kisses and hugs. This helps to relax them from the stresses of the day. They bond together, feeling those fluttery butterfly feelings that made them know they were in love and wanted to be together.

Male birds are known to sing songs, dance, flutter, and walk in special ways to attract the female birds they want to raise a family with. Time and effort should always be put into this bonding time. It is key to keeping Mom and Dad happy and growing together over their many years of marriage, before and after they have their babies.

Once Mom and Dad are feeling relaxed and happy together, their bodies start to respond. Dad's penis starts to prepare for the fertilizer mixing and moving in his testicles, where the sperm is produced.

He and Mom lie very close, and this allows them to come together the way God intended to make you! Her body is warm and receives Dad's fertilizer from his penis into her vagina, a muscular canal that leads from the outside of her body to her uterus. This canal produces a lubrication that allows Dad's sperm to have a warm environment. Sperm are easily able to swim inside her from her vagina to the uterus and eventually the egg.

God designed this to be a happy and enjoyable experience for Mom and Dad as they bond together to create you!

Therefore, a man shall leave his father and his mother and hold fast to his wife, and they shall become one flesh (Genesis 2:24 ESV).

Once ready, Dad's penis releases the semen containing the millions of sperm inside Mom's vagina, and the race to the uterus and the egg begins!

Now, it becomes a long-distance race of the fittest, fastest sperm. To swim up the vagina, through the cervix, into the uterus, around the bend, and finally into the canal called the fallopian tube. Here it finds the egg that Mom's ovary has released that month. The first sperm to reach the egg with Dad's DNA information must push its way inside the covering of the egg with Mom's DNA. And then, ta-da—the winner becomes you!

God allows your journey of growth to becoming a beautiful, healthy baby to begin.

You will have traits from both your mom and dad. Will you have Dad's eye color and Mom's hair color? Will you be big and tall like Dad or short like Grandma? Her information is in there too. DNA traits from both sides of your family for many generations are contained in the egg and the sperm. That is why even though you and your siblings have the same two parents, you are all quite different. God made each one an individual, with different likes, dislikes, eye color, hair color, hair texture, height, and weight. Just like snowflakes, each person is unique with his or her own path provided by God, if they choose to follow it.

> For we are his workmanship, created in Christ Jesus for good works, which God prepared beforehand, that we should walk in them (Ephesians 2:10 ESV).

The whole process is so exciting! Nine months from now, Mom and Dad will get to meet the little blessing God has growing inside Mom's uterus.

Did you know that if more than one sperm and egg combine at the same time or a single fertilized egg splits in half, you get twins? If three combine or a fertilized egg splits into three, you get triplets or even more. Oh my! Mom and Dad could get a boy and a girl in one pregnancy. Being an identical twin myself, I believe multiples are just a bigger blessing from God. More work at one time, but still a blessing.

Now back to the process. The fertilized egg continues its journey down the fallopian tube to Mom's uterus. There it securely plants into the wall of her uterus like a seed is planted into the soil.

As with the seed in soil, God provides the egg with all the food and nutrients the baby will need to grow from the uterus and placenta. The placenta is an organ that develops in Mom's uterus with you. As you grow bigger, the placenta provides you with oxygen to breathe and nutrients needed to grow into a healthy baby. It also helps with removing waste products from your body. God thought of everything! The placenta attaches to the wall of the uterus, and a cord connects to the baby's abdomen, which later will become your belly button.

As I said before, it takes about nine months, or forty weeks, to grow a fully developed baby. We are going to break it down into the trimesters of three months each. Many exciting developments happen each month as the baby gets bigger and stronger and prepares to come out to meet the family!

Behold, children are a heritage from the Lord,
the fruit of the womb a reward.
(Psalms 127:3 ESV)

First Month, First Trimester

Mom may not even realize she is going to have a baby; her body will begin to give her signs or hints that a special person is coming. You, on the other hand, are quite busy during this month. You grow from the size of a grain of pepper to the size of an orange seed. The parts that are beginning to form are your brain, arms, legs, eyes, nose, and spine.

Second Month

Now your heart is beating strongly. It can be seen and heard on an ultrasound. Your arms have elbows, hands, and fingers. Your tiny legs have knees, feet, and toes. That precious face that identifies you has now formed. You are about an inch long, and one third of that is your head!

Third Month

Your hair is growing, and your ears, eyes, and taste buds have formed. The organs deciding whether you are a girl or a boy are growing, though they are not yet visible on your ultrasound. Will Mom and Dad save it as a surprise or find out ahead of time? You are now about three inches long.

Fourth Month, Second Trimester

You are now six inches long and weigh approximately four ounces. You are sucking, swallowing, and stretching inside your mother's womb (uterus). You now have eyelids, eyebrows, and fingernails. Mom still may not feel you moving around, but she will soon. This is when your parents could find out whether you are a girl or boy.

Fifth Month

Now you have grown to about ten inches long and weigh between eight and sixteen ounces. Your muscles have grown much stronger; Mom can now feel you moving. Your skin has developed a substance to coat and protect it from the amniotic fluid, the liquid that provides you cushion and exchange of nutrients. Your inner ear has formed, allowing you to hear Mom's heartbeat and voice.

Sixth Month

Fat that makes you round and cuddly is starting to form under your skin. Major organs such as your liver and pancreas are growing. You are now twelve inches long and weigh around two pounds. Your fingerprints and toe prints are now visible. Your eyelids begin to part so your eyes can open. If you were born now, you could survive outside Mom's womb with a lot of intensive care help.

Seventh Month, Third Trimester

You are moving frequently now, kicking and pushing out with your hands. You are also hearing sounds outside Mom's belly, such as the voices of your dad or siblings. Though you are in darkness, you can detect bright lights outside the womb. You are now fourteen inches long and weigh three pounds.

Eighth Month

You are preparing to come out to meet everyone. One way is comfortably resting with your head down toward the ground to come out headfirst. Some babies like to be different and make their entry feet first! This is frowned upon by the delivering doctor. You make fewer movements and spend more time resting due to the tight quarters now. At the end of this month, your lungs are fully developed. You may have the hiccups from time to time. Your brain is rapidly developing. You are eighteen inches long and weigh approximately five pounds.

Ninth Month

Now you are twenty-one to twenty-three inches long and weigh in the range of six to ten pounds. Your reflexes are coordinated, so you can blink, close your eyes, turn your head, and respond to sounds, light, and touch. Now you have moved down in Mom's pelvis; this allows her to breathe a little more easily. Your head is facing down toward the birth canal. You are resting more and preparing for your exit.

When God decides, He helps your mom's body prepare to push you out through her vagina (the route you got in there). This is the start of labor.

You made all the delicate, inner parts of my body and knit me together in my mother's womb (Psalm 139:13 NLT).

Meeting Day-Your Birthday

Mom is now very tired and looking forward to meeting the small person who has shared her food, air, liquids, and everything for the last nine months. Dad, your family, and their friends are also excited to meet and finally get to hold you.

Mom's abdomen starts to cramp or spasm as her uterus begins tightening and relaxing; this process of squeezing helps to push you out-similar to the way we push toothpaste out of the tube. But this happens with much more discomfort to Mom. This is called labor and is usually painful.

Mom has this discomfort due to Adam and Eve not listening to God the Father and instead eating the fruit from the forbidden tree of knowledge (Genesis 3:16). Listen to your parents because the consequences of not listening can be very painful. Thankfully, God's mercy allows medication to be available to help Mom with the pain.

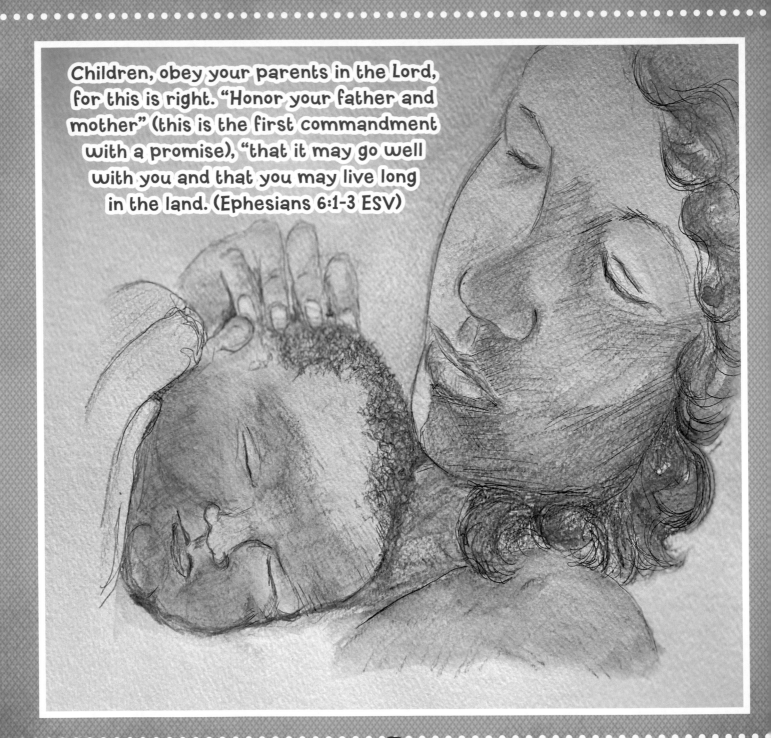

Children, obey your parents in the Lord, for this is right. "Honor your father and mother" (this is the first commandment with a promise), "that it may go well with you and that you may live long in the land. (Ephesians 6:1-3 ESV)

Now back to your meeting day. As the pains become stronger, you push closer to coming to the outside world. Mom uses all her abdominal muscles, squeezing and relaxing over time, to push you out, down from the uterus, through the vagina, and out into the world.

Occasionally, for different reasons, (like those babies trying to enter feet first) things do not work out for Mom to push you out that way. A doctor then performs a surgical procedure in which he or she cuts a small opening in Mom's abdomen and gently pulls you out. No worries—the doctors give Mom some medicine, so this is not too painful for her during the delivery. She must be very careful moving around, carrying you, and other things for a few weeks after.

Once out or delivered, you are quite upset and begin to cry. You have entered a bright, cold, and much louder world than what you had been accustomed to inside the protection of your mom. The doctor carefully snips the cord that has attached you to your mother for many months. When this connection is separated, the small piece of cord left attached to you will dry up and fall off. This leaves you with the belly button you see now.

After a quick cleanup, the doctors and nurses wrap you up tightly in a blanket and give you to Mom and Dad to hug, kiss, and hold. You now clearly hear the voices you have grown to know over the last few months, and God lets you know you are safe and loved.

So God created man in his own image, in the image of God he created him; male and female he created them (Genesis 1:27 ESV).

God has been with you since before you first started growing in your mother's womb, and He will be with you wherever you go as you accomplish His will for your life. You are the masterpiece of His creation; He is your greatest supporter as you discover and live out all that He created you to be. God made each one of us; we were placed in our mothers' womb at the exact time He intended for us to be.

This is the wonderful and miraculous way God provided for you to be made and to get you here. Now you can begin to do all the amazing things God has planned for your life.

Just as God provides everything needed for those little birds and tiny bees, He will always provide for you.

Tonight, and every night before you go to sleep, stop and think about the wonderful miracle of life and about all the special things God did to bring you safely here. Then say thank you to your mom and dad, let them know you love and appreciate them for all they do.

Then send up a special thank you to God, for without His miraculous provision, where would we be if God had not made the birds and the bees?

Printed in the United States
by Baker & Taylor Publisher Services